the ministry of ANGELS & BELIEVERS

by DON GOSSETT

Unless otherwise indicated all Scripture quotations in this volume are from the *King James Version of the Bible.*

Printed in the United States of America
Copyright © 1977 Don and Joyce Gossett
All Rights Reserved

Contents

CHAPTER ONE
The Ministry of Angels............................ 7

CHAPTER TWO
The Ministry of Believers 13

CHAPTER THREE
Your Rights in Christ 19

CHAPTER FOUR
Are You Planning a Nervous Breakdown? 25

CHAPTER FIVE
The Yoke-Breaker 31

Introduction

There are two diverse types of ministries present on the earth today: the ministry of angels and the ministry of believers.

The subject of angels is one about which little is said. The Bible, however, is not silent concerning them. The Psalms tell us of their ministry of protection of God's children: "The angel of the Lord encampeth round about them that fear him, and delivereth them" (Psalm 34:7). "For he shall give his angels charge over thee, to keep thee in all thy ways. They shall bear thee up in their hands, lest thou dash thy foot against a stone" (Psalm 91:11, 12).

As a child of God, you can expect His angels to minister to you. "Be not forgetful to entertain strangers: for thereby some have entertained angels unawares" (Hebrews 13:2).

When Lucifer fell from heaven he took one-third of the angels with him, and they became the foul demons of hell. The remaining two-thirds of heaven's angels are still actively working for God, frequently manifesting their ministry to people today. They do the Lord's work on earth when man's ability is limited.

Often man's ability is limited by his own ignorance. This is where the ministry of believers comes in. First, you must learn what your rights to minister are, and then you must put them into practice.

It is the believer's responsibility to know what the Word of God says about his rights; it is his privilege to exercise those rights, to use the promises in God's Word as his strength for any situation. The tools of a Christian are prayer and praise, used in faith and with boldness.

Discover what your rights are in Jesus and live a successful, powerful, victorious life.

Chapter One
The Ministry of Angels

As David Stuart was about to enter the stream of traffic on Lougheed Highway near Mission City, British Columbia, he saw a man standing at the left front window of his car. "Going to Mission City?" the man asked through the partially-opened window. Since Stuart does not make it a practice to pick up hitchhikers, he ignored the man and proceeded down the highway.

A sincere believer and ardent student of the Word, Stuart was on his way to the Mountain View Church where he was Secretary of the Board. It was the evening of June 13, 1967.

Stuart always drives with his car doors locked. Therefore, he was stunned when after driving about half a mile he looked in his rear-view mirror and saw the hitchhiker sitting in the back seat. "Needless to say," he relates, "I was frozen with fear and could do little but cling to the steering wheel. Eventually I was able to calm down, and I managed to ask, 'Are you a stranger here?'

"To this the man replied, 'I am a stranger to many.'

"No further word was spoken until it was time for me to turn off the highway. I told him I was about to turn left and would have to leave him. As I switched on my turn signal, the man said, 'I just want you to remember one thing: Jesus is coming soon.'

"I turned to reply affirmatively to this, only to find the back seat vacant. I had not stopped my car. No doors had opened or closed. When I arrived at my destination I checked the car doors and found them still locked, as they had been when I left home. I realized that I had been visited by an angel."

The above account is taken from an article which appeared in the magazine, *The Canadian Mennonite,* and is one of several similar reports which have recently come from various western cities.

The ministry of angels has never been given a very large place in Christianity since the time of the Reformation. However, the Bible contains many references to angelic ministries. The Old Testament gives many examples of angelic visits as well as teaching and promise regarding this subject. Angels ministered where man's strength and ability were limited.

In the Gospels there are numerous references to angels. Angels visited Mary and Joseph. Angels announced the Messiah's birth, and at His resurrection they rolled away the stone. They ministered to Jesus in the wilderness. They stood beside the disciples following the

Lord's ascension and told them He was coming back in like manner as they had seen Him go away.

In the Book of Acts we read how an angel opened the prison and delivered the apostles, telling them, "Go, stand and speak in the temple to the people all the words of this life" (Acts 5:20). It was an angel who supernaturally transported Philip from Samaria to Gaza (Acts 8). It was an angel who opened the prison and set Peter free (Acts 12). Throughout the Book of Acts the ministry of angels is evident.

The Book of Acts represents the first 33 years of the Church's ministry, and is the guideline for 20th century Christians. What took place then we have a right to expect today.

In the Book of Acts we see the mighty works of the Spirit through the ministry of the apostles. The instrument they used was the Word of God. The power behind the Word which produced miracles was the name of Jesus. The ability came through the indwelling presence of the Holy Spirit.

Hebrews 1:14 informs us that angels are ministering spirits, sent forth to do service for the sake of them that shall inherit salvation. The conversion of Ed Nelson is a remarkable example of the intervention of angels to reach one who was seemingly destined for a Christless grave.

Ed had always been a hard drinker. One night he was kicked out of a saloon in South Boston after the disgusted bartender told him to go drown himself. Discouraged and broken, Ed walked down to the wharf and leaped into the water.

When he came to the surface he felt a strong hand grip him by the shoulders and lift him bodily out of the water. Not a word was spoken. The stranger pushed him toward the land, but Ed struggled free and jumped into the water again.

Once again these same strong hands grasped him, lifted him out of the water, and this time led him to shore.

Ed knew he had been rescued by an angel. Even in his despondent drunken state he knew that a mighty, unseen force was at work in his life. Bewildered by his miraculous rescue, he returned to the saloon. But not to drink. He only stood by the stove until his clothes were dry and pondered his life.

The next night Ed went to a local mission and gave his heart to Christ.

Ed Nelson's testimony is a remarkable story of the ministry of angels today. This man was later greatly used of God in singing gospel songs and vividly sharing the amazing story of his rescue by an angel.

One of the greatest ministries to be raised up by God in this century was that of William W. Freeman — a ministry born entirely of the supernatural power of God. An ordinary pastor, William Freeman would probably never have been known outside his own circle had it not been for the angelic visitation which changed his life — and ultimately mine.

William Freeman tells of it in this way:

"In the light, an angel suddenly appeared. He was large and wore a white robe. His appearance was strong and his vision penetrating. He touched my body and then told me that God had sent him to give me a gift of healing. I was to go to His people and warn them, tell them that Jesus was coming very soon and that they were sleeping and slumbering. They must be awakened, for great darkness was already upon the land. I was told that I should be diligent and faithful and make haste. He then told me the way I would know when people were being healed."

In almost every prayer of deliverance for the afflicted, Freeman would remind the Lord "what the angel said and told me."

God also gave him visions of vast auditoriums in many parts of the world that would be filled. Later when we walked into an empty auditorium prior to a meeting he would say, "Yes, this will be filled. God showed me it would be filled."

In 1949 God spoke to William Freeman concerning me: "Invite Don Gossett to travel with you in your ministry, for he will do you good." So it was that for seven years of my young life I traveled with this man who had been visited by angels. Together we saw thousands saved and healed through this miraculous ministry.

Chapter Two
The Ministry of Believers

Two weeks before Billy Graham is scheduled to conduct a crusade in a city, a little-known, unofficial member of the Graham team — a spry great-grandmother of 78 — checks into a hotel in that city. She devotes herself to a task undertaken in a vow to God after she was healed of a throat ailment 20 years before. Her job: To pray.

The prayers of Mrs. Pearl Goode of Pasadena, California, together with those of thousands of other prayer partners, may well be the secret weapon of Billy Graham's success as an evangelist. The beginning of her prayer ministry coincides with Graham's emergence as a nationally-known figure. Yet hers has been virtually a hidden ministry.

Mrs. Goode has traveled thousands of miles, mostly by bus, to hundreds of crusades. She rents an inexpensive hotel room, arises by five o'clock each morning to pray, and often continues praying into the night. Before the meetings she goes to the empty auditorium and prays over the pulpit, the empty chairs and the people who will be seated in them.

With tears running from her closed eyes and the light of God clearly shining on her face, she prays, "I pray

God will so fill Billy, anoint his lips, let it flow out of him, that he won't know what he's saying, but that it will be the Holy Spirit speaking through him." Team members ask her to pray for special needs. "But mostly," she says, "God lays it on my heart and I just pray it out."

When Graham went to England Mrs. Goode sensed in prayer that he had a special need, that a trial would come to him. Concerned, she wrote him, "Whatever happens, be a man of the Spirit. Just keep in the Spirit." This was when Graham was troubled by an eye infection which threatened his career.

Mrs. Goode helps conduct the prayer meetings during the crusades and she writes letters to prayer groups. She has been invited to sit on the platform, but she replied, "Then I can only see his back. I want to be in front where I can see him and pray, pray, pray!"

It was in 1949 that Mrs. Goode, a practical nurse saved as a girl in a Methodist revival, first heard the then unknown evangelist. She says, "The Lord gave me a vision of this young man, with his bright tie and bright socks, preaching all over the world. He told me to prepare the way for him by prayer. A friend told me, 'You're crazy. He's just an ordinary man.' But the Lord knew better."

Shortly after this Mrs. Goode was brought close to death by calcium deposits in her throat which made it impossible for her to eat. Doctors told her the deposits could only be removed by surgery. In bed, suffering excruciating pain, she prayed, "Lord, take me home if it is your will. But if you heal me, I'll devote myself to prayer for Billy Graham. I'll go to his crusades and hide away in prayer."

When she arose she felt what she describes as "a wind on my throat." She coughed and caught in her hand what appeared to be a large, jagged pebble. Later, x-rays showed that she was entirely free of the deposits. Her doctors were amazed.

Graham did not know about her until seven years after her vow. But he says he knows when she is in a city — and when she is not. For years now Mrs. Goode has preceded the Graham team from city to city. Her financial needs are somehow always provided.

Prayer is perhaps the most important ministry of believers. When a believer learns what are his rights — and responsibilities — in Christ, he can accomplish anything through the power of prayer.

I constantly carry a burden to help the sick and troubled people whom I meet to find their deliverance.

Daily my mail tells of the most touching needs. Every one of these are calls for prayer. My wife and I, together with our staff, talk directly to God and pray earnestly that He will meet these needs.

Every time I present these requests to the Lord I realize how much it would mean if the people asking for prayer knew certain Bible facts concerning their rights in redemption. If you need healing or liberty from some oppression of the devil, I urge you to consider your rights in Christ.

Recognize that until the victory is fully manifested you are engaged in a fight of faith — a struggle, a battle. A battle of believing against symptoms which would discourage you or which contradict what you believe. Too many people think that if they just had enough faith, all would be easy and everything would be fixed as though some magic wand had been waved over them. A study of faith in the Bible, however, reveals that the man of faith believes God against all kinds of odds and circumstances. His prayers are answered as a result of persistent faith because he is fully convinced that what God promised is true, regardless of circumstances.

So I urge you to face the scriptures squarely and make a decision once and for all whether what you are seeking is God's will for you. Then act on that decision.

If it's in the Word, it's yours. When you are quoting God's Word, you can be as bold as the Word.

Matthew 8:17 says, ". . . Himself took our infirmities, and bare our sicknesses." That includes you. This scripture declares that those physical burdens you carry were taken by Christ. You need not beg Him to do that which is already done. Look at this verse, memorize it, and then look up into the face of Christ, talk directly to Him, and thank Him personally for taking your diseases and weaknesses.

While you look into His face, picture Him as He was stretched to a whipping post, His back bared and bleeding as a Roman soldier plowed furrows on His body with a whip. As you remember Him there, hear the lash of the cat-o'-nine-tails as it slashes through the air and strikes His back. As you think upon the terrible suffering of our Lord you will hear the Holy Spirit say to you, "Through the lashings of that whip and the groans of the Saviour, He suffered our pains and carried our diseases, and with His stripes we are healed."

Then you will be facing the facts of your rights in Christ. They will become real to you as you affirm that "Himself took our infirmities, and bare our sicknesses." You will begin to see them as actual truths instead of just a healing theory. Don't embrace a healing theory, but embrace the reality of Jesus and what He died to provide for you. Let the Spirit of God administer the reality of that to you. For He was beaten for you. He bore your sickness, He took your weakness. The truth of this will grip you deeply as you meditate upon the provision of our Lord and what it cost Him to provide healing for you.

This is God's covenant declaring that you are already healed because Christ took your diseases. Only Satan would burden you with a disease which Christ has already borne for you. Jesus proved that He wants you to be well (III John 2). But you are in the midst of a battle. Satan is opposing you, but God has provided for your deliverance. You have to claim that deliverance as your right.

You must make the decision: This sickness or oppression is of Satan, so it cannot stay. Christ took it. You are free, you are healed. It must be true, so claim it. You will not be denied.

Jesus paid for your health, it belongs to you. You need not fear this thing. It cannot destroy you because Jesus destroyed it for you. Resist the work of Satan. Jesus is in you. He has lifted your load. He is your strength, your health, your life. By His stripes you are healed — now!

Chapter Three
Your Rights In Christ

It is important that you know what belongs to you in Christ and how to possess these rights by faith. Jesus said, "And ye shall know the truth, and the truth shall make you free" (John 8:32). In other words, "When you understand your rights, you can enjoy your liberty."

Without knowing your rights, you may be constantly tormented by fears and uncertainties, by doubts and defeat, by sickness and infirmities. When you know your rights in Christ, you can face each day with certainty. You can act with assurance, you can pray with confidence, you can speak with authority. Your countenance is settled, your attitude is unwavering, your integrity is unblemished.

When you know your rights, your faith does not waver. "But let him ask in faith, nothing wavering. For he that wavereth is like a wave of the sea driven with the wind and tossed. For let not that man think that he shall receive any thing of the Lord. A double minded man is unstable in all his ways" (James 1:6-8).

When you know your rights, you are not willing for Satan or anyone to prevent you from enjoying them. James 4:7 says, ". . . Resist the devil, and he will flee from you." When you know your rights, you will not give up until you possess what is yours in Christ Jesus. The apostle Paul said, ". . . For all things are yours . . . And ye are Christ's; and Christ is God's" (I Corinthians 3:21, 23).

What, then, are some of your rights as a follower of Christ?

1. *You have a right to be saved and free from condemnation*. Thousands are tormented by inward fears that they might not be right with God. This fear continually destroys their faith and steadfastness in prayer. Such tormenting fear is of the devil.

When you accept Christ as your Saviour, understand that He bore your sins and paid the penalty for them. When you confess Jesus before men and tell what He has done for you, you are accepted by our wonderful God. By His creative power, He works a miracle in your life and you are born again. You become a new creature. You are saved. You are changed. His life becomes your life. You are a son of God, your sins are gone, your nature is changed. You are counted as one of God's children. Christ's life, His love, His righteousness begins to be reflected in you.

Yes, you are a Christian; that is, you have become "Christ-like." Such an experience is a miracle of redemption, a marvel of divine love.

This love-life, peace-life, faith-life and health-life is the object of Satan's greatest jealousy. He yearns to destroy such a life. Since he cannot legally affect your salvation, his aim is to undermine your confidence and faith, to torment and accuse you. Satan despises your rights as a believer. He knows that only by affecting your faith can he affect your life with Jesus.

Claim your rights in Christ and allow God's peace to replace the fear and condemnation that once filled your heart.

2. *You have a right to peace.* You are free from your sins because Jesus paid for them. He did not come to condemn the world but that the world through Him might be saved (John 3:17). "Beloved, if our heart condemn us not, then have we confidence toward God" (I John 3:21). If the devil can torment you and condemn you, he knows your confidence is shattered and without faith you will never enjoy the blessings which Jesus died to provide for you.

When Jesus left this earth and returned to the right hand of the Father, He said, "Peace I leave with you, my peace I give unto you . . ." (John 14:27). That peace is yours now. Don't let the devil throw a blanket of condemnation over your soul every time you claim God's blessings. Moffatt's translation of Romans 8:34 reads:

"When God acquits, who shall condemn, when Christ, Who is at God's right hand, actually pleads for us?" You have been acquitted by God, and no devil can condemn you. Jesus will never condemn you because He has provided for your redemption.

I have seen Satan cheat people out of countless blessings by his cunning trick of condemnation. That is why Paul shouts, "There is therefore now no condemnation to them which are in Christ Jesus, who walk not after the flesh, but after the Spirit" (Romans 8:1).

You can say, "Never again will I confess condemnation, for there is now no condemnation to them which are in Christ. I am in Christ; therefore, I am free from condemnation!"

Speak these words: "Therefore being justified by faith, we have peace with God through our Lord Jesus Christ" (Romans 5:1).

One of the fruits of the Spirit is peace (Galatians 5:22).

Ephesians 2:14 says, "For he is our peace. . . ."

Paul commands us, "Let the peace of God rule in your hearts . . ." (Colossians 3:15).

You see, fear and condemnation have no part in a believer. They are of Satan. Resist these wrong spirits and claim the peace of the Lord. For it is yours.

3. *You have a right to be well and strong.* Health belongs to you just as peace does because, ". . . Himself took our infirmities, and bare our sicknesses" (Matthew 8:17).

Sickness is of the devil. It steals energy and health, it loses money and time, it prevents pleasure, and it even kills.

Satan has no right to place disease and weakness on your body. You have a covenant right to health. God's covenant with believers states that the Lord is our physician. "I am the Lord that healeth thee" (Exodus 15:26).

Disease was part of the curse for disobedience. But you are no longer disobedient when you obey the gospel and receive Jesus as Saviour and Lord. Jesus bore your diseases for you (Matthew 8:17; Isaiah 53:5). This is a clear Bible fact. He took your place and bore your punishment of sickness which you deserved to bear. He suffered that you might be healed.

Jesus demonstrated this same covenant in His attitude while on earth by healing every person who sought His healing. Healing was an integral part of every disciple's ministry. The early Christians ministered healing to the sick. The Holy Spirit placed gifts of healing in the Church. An established ordinance of the Church states, "Is any sick among you? let him call for the elders of the church; and let them pray over him, anointing him with oil in the name of the Lord: And the prayer of faith shall save the sick, and the Lord shall raise him up . . ." (James 5:14, 15).

The only reason sickness has been able to invade the lives of countless devout Christians is that Satan has succeeded in making them believe that sickness is from God and will in some way do them some good. The fact is that sickness is entirely of the devil. Jesus healed all who were oppressed of the devil (Acts 10:38).

You have a right to be well. You have a right to have a strong body. Claim your rights. Don't let Satan undermine your faith. Resist him in Jesus' name and he will flee from you (James 4:7). "According as his divine power hath given unto us all things that pertain unto life and godliness . . ." (II Peter 1:3). Sickness pertains to death, for it is death in its premature form. But health pertains to life. God says, "Beloved, I wish above all things that thou mayest prosper and be in health, even as thy soul prospereth" (III John 2).

Claim all your rights. Jesus suffered and died to provide them. Purpose to enjoy them. Resolve to possess what His suffering paid for. Do not yield what belongs to you. Jesus, your victor, stands for you. His peace, health and life are yours today.

Chapter Four

Are You Planning A Nervous Breakdown?

"It seems almost everyone I meet has just had a nervous breakdown, is in the midst of a nervous breakdown, or else is planning to have a nervous breakdown!" So said the Reverend Jack Hyles, pastor of First Baptist Church, Hammond, Indiana. I agree with Pastor Hyles. Nervous breakdowns have reached almost epidemic proportions in our country today, and have become one of the most serious problems currently confronting the medical profession.

One doctor has said that while medical science has conquered many of the deadly diseases which plagued us many years ago, doctors today are facing new illnesses that are just as devastating. Numerous people have fallen victim to these illnesses as a result of the pressures of modern living. They cannot cope with the complexities of our society.

Years ago I was with an older minister and his wife in a home where we were praying for a woman who had suffered a nervous breakdown. These wise, experienced ministers were speaking to the woman's condition as over and over they affirmed the words of Jesus, "Peace, be still." As they kept repeating these life-giving, life-mending words, "Peace be still," the room was flooded with a peaceful, tranquil atmosphere. The woman responded to the peace of the gospel, and her nervous condition improved immediately.

When during a visit to Israel I had the opportunity of sailing on the Sea of Galilee, I thought how Jesus faced that tempestuous sea long ago. The storm, the fears of His disciples, and the turbulence of those waters were a challenge to Him. Yet He simply spoke, "Peace, be still," and the waters became as calm as a sleeping baby.

Your nervous system may be as troubled as those waters of Galilee were. You may be drowning in inner turmoil. The storms, the pressures, the problems of life may overwhelm you. Yet there is intervention through Jesus Christ our Lord. The words of Jesus are spirit and they are life (John 6:63). Hear Him speak to you today, "Peace, be still."

Just as Jesus had complete dominion over the winds and the waves on the Sea of Galilee, so He has complete dominion over you, your body, your nervous system. When you speak His words, it is actually the Master of Galilee speaking through you. For did not He say, "The works that I do shall he (the believer) do also?"

Although we are not facing boisterous waves today on an actual sea, we are facing defeat, fearful situations, sorrow. And like the disciples of Jesus, at times we are at the point of desperation. But know that Jesus is with you even as He was on that fishing boat in Galilee. He has said, ". . . I will never leave you nor forsake you" (Hebrews 13:5); and ". . . Lo, I am with you alway, even unto the end of the world" (Matthew 28:20).

Remember that you are God's child. You were not made for a life of nervous disorder, for frequent bouts with unruly nerves. You were not designed to live a fearful existence. You are God's child and He loves you. Learn to roll your burdens upon Jesus. Visualize yourself literally placing your problems, your difficulties and care, into His hands. He is a big, loving God, and He has big, kind, capable hands.

Perhaps you have heard it said that no child of God ever needs to have a nervous breakdown or be committed to a mental hospital. This is true — with one condition attached. No child of God who practices a positive praise life will ever have a nervous breakdown or be committed to a mental hospital. For when you joyfully praise God, you are dispelling the negative forces that produce nervous breakdowns.

A dear Christian who had suffered from a nervous problem wrote to me recently saying, "For more than three years I have been plagued by a severe nervous problem. I have hesitated to say it was a complete nervous breakdown for I have proudly tried to avoid that term. Perhaps it has been a nervous breakdown. At least, it has been a tormenting time for me and for my dear family.

"I was encouraged by some friends to tune in to your program. I can hardly express in words the help I have received through your ministry. Mainly, your emphasis on praise-power has helped me immensely."

Most nervous problems are caused by the "CDT's." What are the CDT's, you might ask. Some new modern disease? No, it is not exactly a modern condition, although it has grown in prominence in recent times. The CDT'S simply stand for "Cares, Difficulties and Troubles." It is learning to cope with the CDT's of life that brings to many a real challenge of faith.

Here is how you can overcome a nervous disorder by practicing God's order:

1. "Casting all your care upon him; for he careth for you" (I Peter 5:7). Do you have a lot of problems, cares and difficulties today? Don't carry them in your own mind, on your own shoulders. Cast them upon the Lord. Let go of them and let God have them. And leave them with Him.

2. Picture your nervous disorder as like the tempestuous Sea of Galilee with its boisterous, rolling waves. Arise in the name of your Saviour and speak to those nerves as Jesus did to that sea: "Peace, be still." There is amazing power in those words. They are the words of the mighty Creator Himself speaking to His creation. So speak them today.

3. Praise the Lord. Praise elevates your soul to that lofty realm where the Spirit of God is soaring. Praise is in harmony with God's complete expectation of your good life. Discipline your lips to praise the Lord. "By him therefore let us offer the sacrifice of praise to God continually, that is, the fruit of our lips giving thanks to his name" (Hebrews 13:15).

So many people who have nervous trouble are prone to complaining, to seeking justification for their condition. You must stop such negative, gloomy talk or you will never be set free. That is why I stress: Discipline your lips to praise the Lord.

This is God's remedy for a nervous breakdown. Try God's way and experience for yourself His deliverance.

Chapter Five
The Yoke-Breaker

The anointing of the Holy Spirit is given to us to loose every yoke of bondage that Satan may try to put upon us. ". . . The yoke shall be destroyed because of the anointing" (Isaiah 10:27).

Jesus announced at the beginning of His ministry: "The Spirit of the Lord is upon me, because he hath anointed me to preach the gospel to the poor; he hath sent me to heal the brokenhearted, to preach deliverance to the captives, and recovering of sight to the blind, to set at liberty them that are bruised, To preach the acceptable year of the Lord" (Luke 4:18, 19). It was the anointing of the Holy Spirit in Jesus' life that enabled Him to be the liberator of Satan's captives. This same anointing has been given to us that we might minister deliverance to every captive of fear, sickness and condemnation.

This, then, is the key to the ministry of the believer: To have the power of the Holy Spirit dwelling in our lives at all times, ready to do battle with demonic forces.

Do you have trouble reading and understanding the Word of God? Ask the Holy Spirit to illuminate those words to your mind so they will become living words, meaningful and applicable to your life. When the Word of God becomes real to you, you will hunger after it. You will be impelled to study and know its truths. Then you will know what your rights and responsibilites are as a believer.

Then ask the Holy Spirit to reveal to you what are the problem areas in your life and how to use your new-found power to overcome them. "For we wrestle not against flesh and blood, but against principalities, against powers, against the rulers of the darkness of this world, against spiritual wickedness in high places. Wherefore take unto you the whole armor of God, that ye may be able to withstand in the evil day, and having done all, to stand" (Ephesians 6:12, 13).

The yoke-breaker is the Holy Spirit and His tools in your life are the girdle of truth, the breastplate of righteousness, the shoes of preparation, the shield of faith, the helmet of salvation, and the sword of the Spirit, which is the Word of God (Ephesians 6:14-17).